BIOGRAPHY

NATHANAEL GREENE

The General Who Saved the Revolution

FORGOTTEN HEROES
OF THE AMERICAN REVOLUTION

Forgotten Heroes of the American Revolution

NATHANAEL GREENE

The General Who Saved the Revolution

Gregg A. Mierka

OTTN PUBLISHING
STOCKTON, NJ

DEDICATION: This book is dedicated to veterans of all of America's wars and conflicts throughout history.

Frontispiece: A sword owned by Nathanael Greene, one of the greatest generals of the American Revolution.

OTTN Publishing
16 Risler Street
Stockton, NJ 08859
www.ottnpublishing.com

First printing

1 3 5 7 9 8 6 4 2

Library of Congress Cataloging-in-Publication Data

Mierka, Gregg A.
   Nathanael Greene : the general who saved the Revolution / Gregg A. Mierka.
      p. cm. — (Forgotten heroes of the American Revolution)
   Summary: "A biography of the general whose successful campaign in the South, in
what seemed an impossible situation, turned the tide of the American Revolution
and led to a Patriot victory"—Provided by publisher.
   Includes bibliographical references and index.
   ISBN-13: 978-1-59556-012-4 (hc)
   ISBN-10: 1-59556-012-2 (hc)
   ISBN-13: 978-1-59556-017-9 (pb)
   ISBN-10: 1-59556-017-3 (pb)
   1. Greene, Nathanael, 1742-1786—Juvenile literature. 2. Generals—United
States—Biography—Juvenile literature. 3. United States. Continental
Army—Biography—Juvenile literature. 4. Quakers—United
States—Biography—Juvenile literature. 5. United States—History—Revolution,
1775-1783—Juvenile literature. I. Title.

   E207.G9M54 2007
   973.3'3092—dc22
   [B]

                                    2006021044

Publisher's Note: All quotations in this book come from original sources, and contain the spelling and grammatical inconsistencies of the original text.

TABLE OF CONTENTS

Why Nathanael Greene Should Be Remembered

"Greene is as dangerous as Washington. I never feel secure when I am encamped in his neighborhood. He is vigilant, enterprising, and full of resources."

—General Charles Cornwallis, 1781

"It is with a pleasure, which friendship only is susceptible of, that I congratulate you on the glorious end you have put to hostilities in the Southern States; the honour and advantage of it, I hope, and trust, you will live long to enjoy."

—George Washington, letter to Nathanael Greene, February 6, 1783

"What was to be hoped from a general without troops, without magazines, without money? A man of less depth of penetration or force of soul than Greene, would have recoiled at the prospect [of assuming command of the Southern Department of the Continental Army]; but he, far from desponding, undertook the arduous task with firmness. . . . He knew how much was to be expected from the efforts of men contending for the rights of man. He knew how much was to be performed by capacity, courage, and perseverance."

—Alexander Hamilton, eulogy to Nathanael Greene, delivered before the Society of the Cincinnati, July 4, 1789

"But Greene was second to no one in enterprise, in resource, in sound judgment, promptitude of decision, and every other military talent."

—Thomas Jefferson, letter to William Johnson, October 27, 1822

"The great and good man to whose memory we are paying a tribute of respect, affection, and regret, has acted in our revolutionary contest a part so glorious and so important that in the very name of Greene are remembered all the virtues and talents which can illustrate the patriot, the statesman, and the military leader. . . ."

—Marquis de Lafayette, remarks at the dedication of a monument to Greene in Savannah, Georgia, March 21, 1825

"Greene literally appeared out of nowhere to become in the words of one soldier 'the greatest military genius' of the war for independence."

—Theodore Thayer, in *George Washington's Generals and Opponents: Their Exploits and Leadership*, edited by George Athan Billias (1994)

"Nathanael Greene has long been regarded by students of the War of the Revolution as second only to Washington, and the great Virginian considered him his successor if he should be struck down. . . . He was a superb field commander, saw much action, and often risked his life in battle. . . . He made his mark as a brilliant strategist. . . . He was also a military craftsman whose mastery of geography, supply, and transport was unmatched by his contemporaries."

—John Buchanan, in *The Road to Guilford Courthouse: The American Revolution in the Carolinas* (1999)

"In becoming one of the Continental army's greatest soldiers, Nathanael Greene personified the power and potential of the new American idea—especially its rejection of the Old World's aristocratic governments and equally aristocratic military commanders, and its embrace of merit and virtue as society's ultimate arbiters."

—Terry Golway, in *Washington's General* (2005)

"Greene was no ordinary man. He had a quick, inquiring mind and uncommon resolve. He was extremely hardworking, forthright, good-natured, and a born leader. His commitment to the Glorious Cause of America, as it was called, was total. . . . Washington had quickly judged Nathanael Greene to be 'an object of confidence.' "

—David McCullough, in *1776* (2005)

"A GREAT &
GOOD MAN
INDEED"

This monument to Nathanael Greene stands at Guilford Courthouse National Military Park in North Carolina. Although Greene never won a clear victory in battle against the British, his strategy in the South enabled the Americans to win the Revolution.

1

It is said that, after the Revolutionary War, a distraught King George III wished to study the faces of the Americans who had defeated him. His advisers brought portraits of only two men: George Washington and Nathanael Greene.

More than 220 years have passed since the United States won its independence from Great Britain, and the name of Nathanael Greene has largely been forgotten. Yet this Rhode Islander's contributions to the success of the American cause rank with those of the best-remembered heroes of the Revolution: Washington, John Adams, Thomas Jefferson, Benjamin Franklin.

During his time, **Patriots** readily acknowledged the extraordinary debt their country owed to Nathanael Greene. And they felt keenly the nation's loss when, just three years after the end of the Revolutionary War, Greene died at the age of 44. "He was great as a soldier, greater as a citizen, immaculate as a friend," noted General Anthony Wayne, who had served under Greene's command. "The honors, the greatest honors of war, are due to his memory."

"How hard is the fate of the United States to lose such a man in the middle of life!" lamented Lieutenant Colonel Henry "Light Horse Harry" Lee, Greene's cavalry commander, in a letter to George Washington.

But perhaps it was Washington himself who best summed up the life of his friend, adviser, and most trusted general. Of the late Nathanael Greene, the future first president of the United States said simply, "He was a great & good man indeed."

2

EMERGENCE OF A PATRIOT

Nathanael Greene was born on July 27, 1742, at his family's homestead in the village of Potowomut, Rhode Island Colony. He was the second of five sons of Mary Mott Greene, his father's second wife. His father, Nathanael Greene Sr., also had several children by his first wife, who had died young.

Life was often difficult for people living in Great Britain's American colonies during the 18th century. The Greene family was no exception. Nathanael and his brothers (Jacob, William, Elihue, Christopher, and Perry) and stepbrothers (Benjamin and Thomas) all grew up working from dawn to dusk, six days a week, in their father's businesses. Before he turned 12, Nathanael would see the deaths of both of his stepbrothers, his stepsister, his baby sister, and his mother.

A LOVE OF LEARNING

Young Nathanael Greene—called "Natty" by his friends—seems to have been naturally curious. Throughout his life, he would demonstrate a burning desire to learn about a variety of subjects. Nathanael's father appears to have taken a somewhat narrower view of the place of education. Besides being a successful businessman, Nathanael Greene Sr. was a rather strict **Quaker** who led the local congregation. He saw little use for books other than the Bible and a few Quaker texts, and his sons' formal education included only the basics of reading, writing, and mathematics. This, he believed, would provide them with the skills needed to run the family businesses, which included a sawmill, a gristmill, and three iron forges, each with its own bellows, chimney, and anvil.

Despite his father's disapproval of "non-Quaker" ideas, Nathanael Greene eventually managed to collect about 300 books on a wide range of subjects. He read his books whenever he had a spare moment—and sometimes when he didn't. Often, while Nathanael was supposed to be tending to some task at the Greene iron foundry, his brothers would find him lost in a book. By the time he reached adulthood, his avid reading had given him a respectable knowledge in many fields of study. His learning even extended to military science—a clear indication that he had drifted away from his strict Quaker upbringing, as Quakers reject

Nathanael Greene was born in this house in Rhode Island in 1742. The Old Forge Homestead, as it is known, was built in 1684.

violence and war as a means of settling disputes. In spite of the impressive range of his self-taught knowledge, Nathanael Greene would always be somewhat self-conscious about his lack of formal schooling. In a letter to his good friend Samuel Ward Jr., he wrote, "I lament the want of a liberal Education; I feel the mist [of] Ignorance to surround me."

SEEDS OF THE REVOLUTION

During Nathanael's teenage years, as he strove to educate himself while learning the trade of ironmaster at his father's forge, war raged in North America. Neither the Greene family nor the Rhode Island Colony was directly involved in the fighting. But the conflict—called the French and Indian War by people in Britain's American colonies—set the stage for later events in which Nathanael Greene would play an important role.

The French and Indian War was essentially a struggle over whether France or Great Britain would be the dominant colonial power in North America. By 1760, after six years of fighting, the British side had defeated the French side. The victory seemed to guarantee that Britain's North American colonies were secure. In fact, the seeds of rebellion were about to be sown.

The French and Indian War had cost the British treasury a huge amount of money. In order to pay off its war debts and make the American colonies more profitable and easier to manage, Britain instituted a series of measures. These included laws enacted by **Parliament** that imposed import **duties** and other taxes on the colonists, such as the Sugar Act of 1764, the Stamp Act of 1765, and the Townshend Acts, passed in 1767. From the point of view of King George III and his advisers, such measures were perfectly legitimate: as subjects of the Crown, the American colonists were bound by whatever laws Parliament saw fit to enact. Besides, it wasn't unreasonable to expect the colonists to help pay for their own defense. American Patriots saw things a little differently: since they weren't permitted to vote in parliamentary elections, Parliament, they believed, didn't have the right to tax them.

Unrest in the colonies mounted, though no one as yet entertained the idea of independence from Great Britain. Colonists simply wanted to stop what they regarded as Parliament's infringement on their legitimate rights. Resistance to British authority was especially strong in New England. To maintain order and enforce the collection of His Majesty's customs and taxes, two British regiments were dispatched to Boston. The *redcoats* arrived in 1768.

Tensions between Bostonians and the king's soldiers simmered, finally boiling over in an incident that Patriots would dub the Boston Massacre. On March 5, 1770, an angry mob gathered in front of the customs house and began pelting a small detachment of redcoats with snowballs and ice. As the mob pressed in on them, the soldiers opened fire. After the smoke had cleared, five rioters lay dead. News of the incident (often with the circumstances exaggerated by Patriots) spread throughout the 13 colonies. This fueled more outrage against the British.

THE POLITICAL AWAKENING OF NATHANAEL GREENE

If Nathanael Greene was outraged by the Boston Massacre, there is no indication of that in his surviving correspondence from 1770 and 1771 (including a series of letters to his friend Samuel Ward). Nor do his letters reveal any views about the British policies that were

Paul Revere made this inflammatory engraving of the March 1770 incident that became known as the Boston Massacre. Patriot leaders used the incident to stir up resentment of British policies.

provoking indignation among more radical colonists. But then, personal matters were probably much on Greene's mind throughout this time. His father had earlier assigned him to manage the family's iron factory in the town of Coventry, Rhode Island. Coventry was situated along the south branch of the Pawtuxet River, about eight miles west of Potowomut. Greene designed a new home for himself in Coventry. Spell Hall, as he called the home, was built atop a sparsely wooded hill overlooking the Pawtuxet. It sat on about 85 acres of land, most of which was used for farming and the raising of livestock. After its completion in 1770, Nathanael Greene and his older brother Jacob moved into Spell Hall. Later that year, their father died, and the Greene brothers inherited the family business.

By this time, Nathanael Greene was already one of Coventry's most prominent citizens. In 1768, he had been elected to the first of three terms he would serve in Rhode Island's colonial legislature. In 1770, reflecting his lifelong interest in education, he provided a schoolhouse for the children of his workers.

Greene's gradual transformation into a supporter of American independence may have begun in 1772. Early that year, a British naval vessel, the HMS *Gaspee*, began patrolling Rhode Island waters to prevent smuggling and make sure all the import duties owed to the Crown were paid. The *Gaspee*'s commander, Lieutenant William Dudingston, quickly earned the hatred of Rhode Islanders for harassing merchant vessels and their crews.

In late February, an armed party from the *Gaspee* boarded the merchant vessel *Fortune* as it lay at anchor in Narragansett Bay. The *Fortune*, owned by Nathanael Greene & Co., was carrying a cargo of rum. Dudingston

Spell Hall, the house Nathanael Greene built in Coventry, Rhode Island, is now a museum. The cannon in front of the house was cast during the American Revolution at the Greene family's nearby forge.

declared that the ship was engaged in rum smuggling, confiscated it, and illegally had it taken to Boston. Charges against the Greenes were eventually dropped for lack of evidence, but they were never compensated for the loss of the cargo of rum. Furious, Nathanael Greene filed a lawsuit against Dudingston, and Rhode Island authorities issued a warrant for the British officer's arrest.

Dudingston's abuses were eventually ended not by a judge but by a group of defiant Rhode Islanders. On June 9, 1772, while chasing the merchant ship *Hannah* in

Narragansett Bay, the *Gaspee* ran aground in shallow water. The *Hannah* proceeded to Providence, where its captain shared the news of Dudingston's predicament. That night, Providence men filled eight longboats and rowed out to the stranded warship. Just before dawn on June 10, after taking the crew off the *Gaspee*, the Rhode Islanders set the ship ablaze.

The entire *Gaspee* affair appears to have spurred a political awakening in Nathanael Greene. For the first time, his letters begin to contain pointed observations about the abuses of British authority.

GATHERING STORM

Over the next few years, the American colonies slid toward rebellion. In 1773, Parliament passed the Tea Act, which gave the British East India Company sole rights to sell tea in the colonies. Patriots responded by preventing cargoes of East India Company tea from being unloaded. On the evening of December 16, 1773, a group of Bostonians went a step further. Disguised as Mohawk Indians, they boarded British ships and dumped 342 cases of tea into Boston Harbor. The incident became known as the Boston Tea Party. In 1774, Parliament passed a series of measures to punish Massachusetts for defying the Crown's authority—and to warn other colonies against similar rebelliousness. The measures, which Patriots referred to as the Intolerable Acts,

Small boats filled with angry Rhode Islanders row away as the British warship *Gaspee* burns on a shoal in Narragansett Bay. The destruction of the *Gaspee*, on June 10, 1772, was one of the first cases of violent resistance to the British government by American colonists.

included a law that closed the port of Boston to all trade; a law that changed the government of Massachusetts, replacing elected officials with officials appointed by the king or his royal governor; and a law that forced colonists to provide lodging for British soldiers in private homes.

The harsh treatment of Massachusetts didn't have the effect Parliament intended. Far from frightening other colonies into submission to the Crown, the Intolerable Acts only created sympathy for Massachusetts and moved the colonies toward more unified opposition. The First Continental Congress, with delegates from all the colonies except Georgia, convened in Philadelphia in September 1774 to address the colonies' common grievances against British rule.

By this time, Nathanael Greene was a zealous Patriot. And he believed that the differences between Britain and the American colonies would be settled only by a clash of arms. "Soon very soon," he wrote, "expect to hear the thirsty Earth drinking in the warm Blood of American sons." In anticipation of the coming struggle, Greene helped form a Rhode Island *militia* unit in his home county of Kent. The men called their group the Kentish Guard.

But during the late summer and fall of 1774, Greene's mind was not completely occupied by politics or the prospect of war with the British. In July, the longtime bachelor had married Catharine Littlefield, a beautiful and outgoing young woman from Block Island whom he affectionately called Kitty. He was 32, she 19. Nathanael and Caty, as Catharine was called by friends, would enjoy a few months together at Spell Hall before momentous events pulled him away.

3

THE FIGHTING QUAKER

On April 19, 1775, a column of British soldiers battled swarms of Massachusetts militia units at the villages of Lexington and Concord and throughout a long retreat to Boston. The redcoats suffered more than 270 casualties, including 73 dead. Around 50 Americans were killed in the fighting. Although some people continued to hope that Great Britain and its colonies could be reconciled, the American Revolution had begun.

Lexington and Concord captured the imagination of Patriots everywhere. When the Massachusetts Committee of Safety issued a call for help in protecting the colony's citizens against the British army, militia units from throughout New England answered the call. Soon these Patriots

Redcoats and American militiamen exchange gunfire on Lexington Green, April 19, 1775. After the bloody clashes at Lexington and Concord, Nathanael Greene was prepared to join the Patriot fight as a private (the lowest military rank) in a local militia unit. Within weeks, however, he would be named commanding general of the Rhode Island brigade.

would join their Massachusetts brothers in what was called "the Army of Observation." It deployed in an arc around the port of Boston, keeping the British bottled up in the city.

FROM PRIVATE TO GENERAL

Initially, Rhode Island governor Joseph Wanton dispatched the Kentish Guard to join the Army of Observation. Nathanael Greene had wished to command the unit, but he marched out as a lowly private. As a result of his wide reading on military subjects, Greene probably knew more about strategy and tactics than anyone in the Kentish Guard. He was also a physically imposing man: he stood about 5 foot 10—tall for the era—and was very powerfully built. But when the time had come for the Kentish Guard to elect their leader, they chose someone else. The reason seems rather silly today: Greene walked with a slight limp (possibly the result of a childhood accident), which the men thought would detract from the unit's appearance if he were in command. In the end, Private Greene never reached Boston with the Kentish Guard. Governor Wanton—who was suspected of having *Tory* sympathies—recalled the unit before they had joined the Army of Observation.

Greene was furious with this decision, but he soon got another chance to fight for the cause of liberty. Rhode Island's legislature had approved the formation of a 1,500-man army. On May 8, 1775, Nathanael Greene was appointed the commanding general of the Rhode Island brigade.

Outside Boston, Greene and his men took their place among the Patriots laying siege to the city. In many ways, the assembled Americans were a ragtag bunch. The force lacked strong, unified command. Many of the units were ill equipped, poorly trained, and badly led. Amid the boredom of the siege, their discipline suffered.

From the outset, Nathanael Greene was determined that his Rhode Islanders would not fall prey to lax discipline.

While other units lolled about their camps, drinking and gambling, his men would drill. Men who behaved in a manner unbefitting a soldier would be punished. But Greene also understood that a fighting unit needed more than training and discipline to be effective. It needed adequate supplies of everything from weapons and ammunition to food and blankets. Believing that his men weren't provisioned as well as they should be, he traveled to Providence to prod Rhode Island officials into sending more supplies.

LESSONS OF BUNKER HILL

On June 17, 1775, while Greene was on this trip to Providence, British and American soldiers fought the Battle of Bunker Hill. The bloody engagement took place near Charlestown, just north of Boston. There American rebels had fortified Breed's Hill, and British officers feared that cannons placed on the high ground might threaten parts of Boston or His Majesty's warships in the harbor. Waves of British *regulars* marched directly up the hill, only to be mowed down by rebels firing from behind their fortifications. When the rebels finally ran out of ammunition, they were forced to retreat. The British had won the battle, but at a ghastly price. More than 225 British officers and men had been killed, and nearly 900 more wounded. American casualties were estimated at about 440, including 140 killed.

British troops are shot down as they march uphill toward American fortifications near Boston. The misnamed Battle of Bunker Hill (most of the fighting actually occurred on nearby Breed's Hill) was a costly victory for the British.

Even though Nathanael Greene had missed the Battle of Bunker Hill, he quickly grasped its lesson. In a letter to a friend, he wrote, "I wish we could sell them another hill at the same price we did on Bunkers Hill." In 18th-century European warfare, the side that held the field at the end of a battle was considered the victor. Yet, Greene realized, the British could win a string of battles but still lose the war if the Americans made the cost of the British victories high enough. It was a lesson he would remember throughout his years as a Revolutionary War general.

THE CONTINENTAL ARMY TAKES BOSTON

Only days before the Battle of Bunker Hill, important decisions regarding the future of America's rebel army had been made hundreds of miles to the south, in Philadelphia. The Second Continental Congress, believing that the American cause required more than a hodgepodge of militia units from the various colonies, decided to create a unified force of regular soldiers. To lead the new Continental Army, Congress chose George Washington, a Virginian who had fought in the French and Indian War. Congress also commissioned four *major generals* and eight *brigadier generals*. The youngest of the brigadier generals was Nathanael Greene. The 32-year-old, who would win the nickname "the Fighting Quaker of Rhode Island," had already impressed his older colleagues with his gift for command.

In early July, Washington arrived in Cambridge, Massachusetts, to take command of his army. He was shocked at the dreadful state of affairs he found. There were critical shortages of gunpowder and other supplies, and discipline among many of the Continental units was horrendous. But Washington was impressed by Nathanael Greene, whose Rhode Island brigade may have been the best-trained, best-disciplined, and best-equipped unit in the army. The two men formed an immediate bond of respect, which would grow into a lifelong friendship. Recognizing Greene's talents, Washington ordered him to take command of the Continentals defending Prospect Hill, one of the most important positions during the siege of Boston.

Summer passed, and then fall, but the military situation remained a stalemate. The British weren't willing to risk a full-scale attack on the Continental Army to lift the siege. The Continental Army wasn't strong enough to take Boston by storm. So both sides waited. Conditions for the Patriot soldiers encamped outside Boston weren't pleasant, particularly as the New England winter set in. Many of the soldiers went home after their enlistments expired on January 1, 1776. Greene's brigade shrank to 700 soldiers, less than half of what its strength should have been.

It took heroic action to finally end the stalemate. In the dead of winter, an expedition led by Greene's friend Henry Knox, Washington's commander of artillery, removed 59 cannons from Fort Ticonderoga, in northeastern New York, and dragged the heavy weapons 300 miles across snow and ice all the way back to Boston. On the morning of March 5, the British commander in Boston, Sir William Howe, awoke to see the barrels of the big guns atop Dorchester Heights. When an attempt to dislodge the Americans from their positions failed, he decided to evacuate the city.

American soldiers, commanded by Greene's friend Henry Knox, use sledges to move cannons through the snow to Boston. The cannons, captured at Fort Ticonderoga in May 1775, were used to fortify Dorchester Heights in early 1776. This forced the British to leave Boston.

DEFEAT ON LONG ISLAND

There was little time for celebration, however. The British would launch a major offensive, and the most likely target was New York City.

In early April of 1776, the Continental Army marched from Boston to New York. General Washington placed

Nathanael Greene in command on the strategically vital Long Island, located across the East River from Manhattan Island, site of New York City. This reflected how much the commander in chief had come to trust his young general during the long siege of Boston.

The scope of the challenge facing Greene and the Continental Army became apparent on June 29, when about 100 British warships and troop transport ships sailed into Lower New York Bay and dropped anchor off Staten Island. Large as this armada was, it represented only a part of the British invasion fleet that Sir William Howe was assembling. Eventually about 32,000 soldiers—British regulars as well as **Hessians**—disembarked on Staten Island. There they rested and drilled in preparation for the coming attack on the rebels.

Anxiety filled the ranks of the 19,000-man Continental Army. Many of these men had no military experience. But morale received a big boost on July 9, when Washington ordered the Declaration of Independence read to all the troops. Adopted five days earlier by the Continental Congress, it made clear what the men were fighting for— nothing less than an independent, sovereign United States.

In early August, Congress promoted Nathanael Greene to the rank of major general in the Continental Army. Unfortunately, by the middle of the month Greene had come down with an illness that produced a high fever and

Major General Israel Putnam took over command of American troops on Long Island when Greene became sick. Putnam had earned a reputation as a brave and capable leader during the French and Indian War, and had been a hero at Bunker Hill, but he did not perform well on Long Island.

left him weak and bedridden. Though Greene desperately wanted to resume his duties on Long Island, Washington sent him to Manhattan to recover. In Greene's absence, Washington assigned Major General Israel Putnam to take over as commander on Long Island.

Putnam, less familiar than Greene with Long Island's terrain, failed to establish a defensive position at a critical pass east of the Continental Army's lines. This oversight led to disaster on August 27, when Hessians attacked the front of the Continental lines while redcoats (who had marched through the unguarded Jamaica Pass the night before) struck from the rear. After a chaotic American retreat to Brooklyn Heights, General Washington and the bulk of his army, their backs to the East River, faced annihilation. Fortunately for the Continentals, Howe did not immediately press his advantage. This enabled Washington to evacuate his men across the East River and into Manhattan during the night of August 29 and the morning of August 30. Still, the Battle of Long Island had been a crushing defeat. The Continentals suffered more than 1,400 casualties, the British fewer than 400.

THE FORT WASHINGTON FIASCO

Nathanael Greene was still sick—"scarcely able to sit up an hour at a time," as he informed his brother Jacob in a letter dated August 30, 1776. "Gracious God!" he lamented. "To be confined at such a time."

Though he continued to suffer lingering effects from his illness, Greene had returned to duty by September 15, when Howe renewed his pursuit of the Continental Army. As British warships unleashed a barrage of cannon fire, 10 battalions of redcoats and Hessians crossed the East River and landed on Manhattan Island at a place called Kip's Bay.

A few days earlier, Greene had convinced Washington—and the other major generals of the Continental Army—that the American forces could not successfully defend New York City. The best option was to retreat northward on Manhattan Island. On September 16, when British units

A week after the British occupied New York City in September 1776, a huge fire destroyed at least one-quarter of the city's buildings. The British suspected—with reason, many modern historians believe—that the fire was deliberately set by American Patriots. In this French engraving from 1778, buildings burn while British soldiers beat hapless citizens in the streets and black slaves loot.

made contact with the rear guard of Washington's retreating army, Greene commanded a regiment that helped send the redcoats fleeing in what came to be called the Battle of Harlem Heights. It was a small if heartening victory, but the American retreat northward continued.

Greene made a big mistake when he decided to defend Fort Washington despite the doubts of his commander in chief, the fort's namesake. Fort Washington, perched on a hill overlooking the Hudson River at the northern end of Manhattan Island, sat opposite another stronghold on the New Jersey side of the river, Fort Lee. By holding on to Fort

Washington, Greene hoped to prevent British warships from sailing up the Hudson, as well as to keep large numbers of British soldiers tied down on Manhattan Island. Greene also hoped to lure the British into an assault that would prove as costly to them as Bunker Hill.

The battle at Fort Washington did prove extremely costly—but not to the British. On the morning of November 16, a British force numbering 10,000 attacked the fort. Generals Washington, Greene, Israel Putnam, and Hugh Mercer—who had crossed the river from Fort Lee to assess the situation—were nearly caught up in the swift British assault but managed to escape. The nearly 3,000 men defending Fort Washington weren't so lucky. Those who weren't killed surrendered within a few hours. In addition, the British captured more than 40 cannons and tons of gunpowder. For the Americans, the engagement was a total disaster.

The fiasco at Fort Washington damaged Greene's reputation for a while. It also reflected badly on George Washington, who had taken the advice of his young general. Some Continental officers said that both Washington and Greene should be dismissed in the wake of Greene's blunder. Certain members of Congress appeared inclined to agree. But Washington remained in charge. And while he didn't shield his young general from criticism, he refused to fire Greene. That would turn out to be an excellent decision.

4

A TRAIL OF BLOOD

Retreat and humiliation followed the American army on the heels of the Fort Washington disaster. As many as 5,000 dispirited militiamen from Massachusetts simply left, reducing by half the size of Washington's force. On November 20, thousands of redcoats crossed the Hudson north of Fort Lee, which ultimately had to be abandoned. The demoralized Continental Army was forced to begin a hasty retreat southwest across New Jersey. Washington and his weary men finally reached the banks of the Delaware River north of Trenton. On December 11, they crossed the river into the relative safety of Pennsylvania just ahead of the pursuing British.

But the Revolution seemed doomed to fail. Washington's tattered army, now shrunken to about 2,400 defeated and demoralized men, might virtually disappear with the coming of the new year. That's when most of the one-year Continental Army enlistments were set to expire. The militias could hardly be counted on to carry the banner of liberty, either. During the retreat across New Jersey, George Washington had asked the state militia to turn out to support his regulars. Of the 16,000 men in the state militia, only about 1,000 had answered the call.

WASHINGTON STRIKES BACK

Washington wasn't ready to let the Revolution die, however. As 1776 drew to a close, he gathered Nathanael Greene, Henry Knox, and his other generals together in council. They decided to launch a surprise attack on the 1,400-man Hessian contingent in Trenton. Around nightfall on Christmas, Washington's army began boarding boats to cross the ice-choked Delaware River. By 4 A.M. on December 26, the last of the 2,400 Continentals had been ferried across the river to a point about eight miles north of Trenton. After a march made more miserable by wind-whipped snow and sleet, the ragged army reached the town around 8 A.M. Many Hessians were still sleeping off the effects of their Christmas celebrations when the first American gunfire rang out. They tried desperately to form ranks, but the

Continentals pressed in on them relentlessly. Sometime after nine o'clock, the Hessians surrendered. More than 100 of the German professional soldiers had been killed or wounded in the battle, and 900 were taken prisoner. American casualties totaled only four wounded.

Stunned by the apparent resurgence of a rebellion he thought was all but extinguished, Sir William Howe recalled his best general, Charles Cornwallis, and ordered him to pursue Washington. Cornwallis's baggage had already been loaded on a ship in preparation for his return to England.

This painting shows George Washington leaning against a captured cannon after the Battle of Princeton. Despite Greene's mistakes in New York, Washington did not lose confidence in the younger general. Greene played an important role in the American victories at Trenton and Princeton.

On January 2, the armies of Cornwallis and Washington encountered each other around Trenton. By nightfall, after a series of skirmishes, Cornwallis believed he had the Americans trapped on a hillside. But Washington slipped away overnight and marched to Princeton. There he defeated the British the following day. Cornwallis withdrew his force to New Brunswick, abandoning any notion of a winter campaign to finish off the rebels.

Washington's bold and aggressive action in the final week of 1776 and the first week of 1777 heartened Patriots when it seemed that their cause was hopeless. The Revolution had been saved—at least for the time being.

ENCAMPED AT MORRISTOWN

The American army, depleted and badly in need of provisions, spent the rest of the winter in the hills around Morristown, New Jersey. Months earlier, Greene had sent some men under his command to scout and secure the Morristown area in case the Continental Army had to encamp there during its retreat from New York. Now his gift for planning and organization was paying off—as it would time and again in the coming years.

With the arrival of spring, the British and American forces prepared to resume their struggle. Greene had no illusions about the difficulties and sacrifices that lay ahead for the Continental Army—and for himself. In a letter to

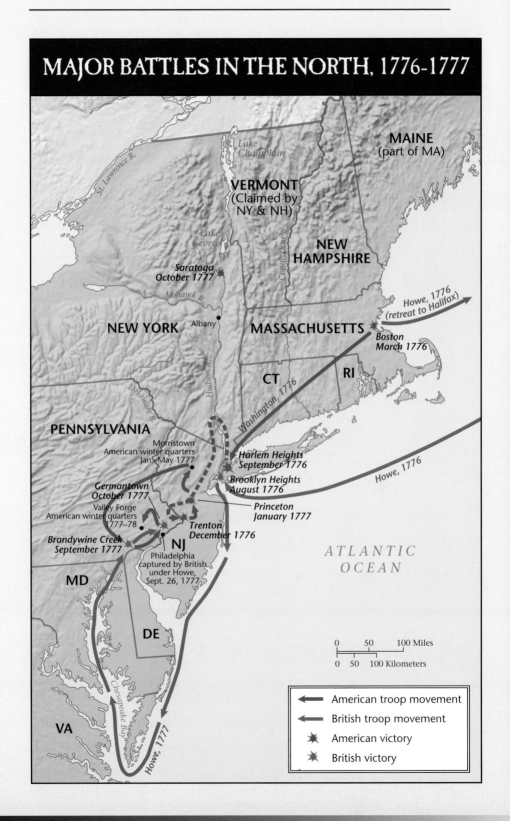

MAJOR BATTLES IN THE NORTH, 1776-1777

St. Lawrence R.

Lake Champlain

MAINE
(part of MA)

VERMONT
(Claimed by
NY & NH)

Lake George

NEW
HAMPSHIRE

Saratoga
October 1777

Howe, 1776
(retreat to Halifax)

Mohawk R.

NEW YORK   Albany

MASSACHUSETTS

Boston
March 1776

Hudson R.

CT   RI

Washington, 1776

PENNSYLVANIA

Delaware R.

Morristown
American winter quarters
Jan.-May 1777

Harlem Heights
September 1776

Brooklyn Heights
August 1776

Howe, 1776

Germantown
October 1777

Valley Forge
American winter quarters
1777–78

Princeton
January 1777

Brandywine Creek
September 1777

Trenton
December 1776

NJ

Philadelphia
captured by British
under Howe,
Sept. 26, 1777

MD

ATLANTIC
OCEAN

DE

| 0 | 50 | 100 Miles |
| 0 | 50 | 100 Kilometers |

VA

Chesapeake Bay

Howe, 1777

⬅ American troop movement

⬅ British troop movement

✴ American victory

✴ British victory

his wife dated April 27, 1777, he wrote, "I long to hear from you but wish more to see you. That happy period I fear is at a great distance. . . . The Campaign I expect will open in a few days . . . we may not see one another for some months." It had already been 10 months since the couple last laid eyes on each other, when Caty visited Long Island before the British offensive. In the meantime, she had given birth to their second child, Martha Washington Greene; George Washington Greene, their son, was now two. Greene ended his letter by lamenting the apathy of much of the American public toward the cause of liberty. "I am sure America will be Victorious finally," he wrote, "but her sufferings for want of Union and public Spirit may be great first. . . . God grant a happy issue to the War. . . ."

"A happy issue to the War" was by no means certain as the summer of 1777 approached. By June the Continental Army had about 9,000 men fit for duty. But Sir William Howe—based in New York City—had 27,000 regulars at his disposal.

THE CAMPAIGNS OF 1777

In June a British force of more than 7,000 invaded New York from Quebec. If that force, under the command of General John "Gentleman Johnny" Burgoyne, linked up with Howe's troops, the British would control all of New

York. This would cut off New England, effectively splitting the rebellious states in two.

But Gentleman Johnny's expedition wasn't all that Washington and his generals had to worry about as 1777 unfolded. In late July, Sir William Howe set sail from New York with about 15,000 redcoats and Hessians, leaving the remainder of his force in New York under the command of Sir Henry Clinton. Though his target was Philadelphia, Howe bypassed the Delaware Bay and sailed up the

Greene's leadership at Brandywine in September 1777 helped save the Continental Army from being destroyed by a superior British force under General William Howe.

Chesapeake. On August 25, the British force reached Head of Elk, Maryland. An overland march of about 60 miles could put Howe at the rebels' capital city.

Washington quickly moved to block the British advance. He marched his army to the banks of Brandywine Creek, southwest of Philadelphia. It should have been a good position to defend. But Washington and his generals expected the British to try to cross the Brandywine at a place called Chad's Ford (now spelled Chadds Ford). Instead, Howe slipped the main body of his force across the creek farther north, at an undefended position. On the afternoon of September 11, British troops descended on the American right flank, which buckled and began to break. Washington ordered Nathanael Greene to march reserve troops north from Chad's Ford to save the right flank. Greene and his men covered the four miles in a remarkable 45 minutes. Taking their positions in the line, Greene's soldiers enabled the Continental Army to make an orderly retreat instead of facing complete destruction. Still, the Americans suffered heavy casualties at the Battle of Brandywine, and the way was now open for the British to take Philadelphia.

On September 26, some 3,000 redcoats under the command of Lord Cornwallis marched into Philadelphia. Congress had earlier fled the city for York, Pennsylvania.

But Washington wasn't prepared to accept a British occupation of Philadelphia without another fight. On

October 4, the Continental Army attempted a surprise dawn attack on the 9,000-man British garrison encamped at the village of Germantown, five miles north of Philadelphia. Nathanael Greene was assigned a major role in the four-column battle plan, but his men got lost on the nighttime march to Germantown and arrived late. While the assault caught Howe off guard, the American attack soon stalled. After inflicting substantial casualties on the British, the Americans wisely retreated.

Continental soldiers are turned back by redcoats holed up inside a stone house owned by the prominent Loyalist Benjamin Chew at the Battle of Germantown. Washington had developed a complex battle plan, but poor timing, heavy fog, and bad luck contributed to an American defeat.

Unable to dislodge the enemy from Philadelphia, Washington's army withdrew to Whitemarsh, Pennsylvania. There they would encamp for the next six weeks.

The news was better from New York. On October 17, at Saratoga, Gentleman Johnny Burgoyne surrendered his surrounded and outnumbered army to the American commanding general, Horatio Gates.

In spite of this development, the American cause again looked bleak as the winter of 1777–78 approached. As the British settled into warm and well-provisioned winter quarters in Philadelphia, George Washington's exhausted and tattered army marched to its winter encampment 25 miles to the west, at a place called Valley Forge. Food was scarce, and many of the Americans lacked warm clothing. Many didn't even have shoes, and, as Washington observed, "you might have tracked the army from White Marsh to Valley Forge by the blood of their feet."

5

THE QUARTER-MASTER GENERAL

If the long march to Valley Forge proved grueling, the weary Continental soldiers found little respite when they limped into the site of their winter camp in mid-December. First they faced a grim race against time. Before the worst of winter set in, hundreds of shelters would have to be constructed to protect perhaps 10,000 men from the bitter cold. Nathanael Greene helped direct the rapid building of small log cabins that housed a dozen men each. They came to be called Greene huts.

But shelter was just one of the critical problems facing Washington's army. The soldiers had to be clothed and, even

During the harsh winter of 1777–78, American soldiers at Valley Forge lived in small log cabins like this. Because Nathanael Greene directed their construction, the buildings became known as Greene huts.

more important, fed. Unfortunately, Congress had allowed the army's supply system to disintegrate. And local merchants and farmers were reluctant to sell their goods to the Continental Army. Some of these Pennsylvania merchants and farmers were Tories. Others believed that the Revolution was doomed to fail and worried about the consequences of supporting the losing side. But for many, the decision was a purely economic one: the value of the Continental dollar was steadily declining. Soon the currency that Congress had established and that the army used to pay its debts might be all but worthless.

By early February, starvation stalked the camp at Valley Forge. With no other options, Washington issued an order permitting his soldiers to seize the supplies they needed and to present farmers with certificates that supposedly could be redeemed later for payment. But this only caused the locals to hide their goods. At this point, Nathanael Greene was placed in charge of the army's *foraging* operation. Lacking a way to transport the supplies his men found, Greene sent a unit west into Lancaster County to bring back 100

Washington reviews troops at Valley Forge. Although farmers had enjoyed record harvests in the fall of 1777, the Continental supply system was so inefficient that the American soldiers at Valley Forge were in danger of starving. To save the army, Washington placed Greene in charge of finding food and supplies.

wagons. He ordered other detachments to fan out into Chester, Montgomery, and Bucks counties in Pennsylvania, and he even sent a unit under the command of General "Mad" Anthony Wayne into New Jersey. He treated uncooperative locals sternly.

Within a few weeks, Greene's efforts had begun to pay off. Livestock, grain, and other supplies trickled into camp. But throughout the rest of the harsh winter, men continued to die for want of food and warm clothes (an estimated 2,500 Continental soldiers perished at Valley Forge).

"OUT OF THE LINE OF SPLENDOR"

Washington recognized that if he still had an army when spring arrived, a long-term problem would have to be addressed. The Continental Army needed a reliable supply system if there was any hope of winning the war. And Nathanael Greene's foraging efforts at Valley Forge only confirmed what Washington already knew: that Greene was the best man to fill the post of **quartermaster general**, the officer in charge of keeping the army provisioned and of scouting and selecting sites for the army to encamp as it moved in the field. From his days managing the iron forge in Coventry, Greene understood how to get supplies where they were needed and at the right time. He was also well acquainted, from his time as a general, with the many requirements of an army in the field. Plus, he was by nature highly organized

Nathanael Greene's signed pledge to faithfully discharge the duties of quartermaster general of the Continental Army, witnessed by George Washington and dated May 23, 1778. Greene accepted the post of quartermaster general only reluctantly.

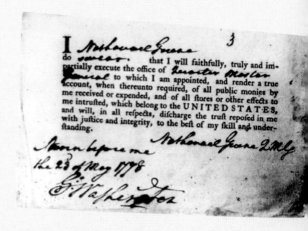

and methodical. On March 2, 1778, Greene was summoned to the commander in chief's headquarters and informed that Congress was going to appoint him to the post of quartermaster general of the Continental Army.

He was less than thrilled by the news. Greene wanted to command troops in battle alongside General Washington, not to spend his days in tedious administrative work. To soften the blow, Washington allowed Greene to retain his rank as a major general, pledged to include him in strategic planning, and promised him an important command by war's end. Greene agreed to accept the position, but he made little attempt to hide his disappointment. On March 9, he wrote to his friend Joseph Reed, "I am taken out of the Line of splendor." In a March 28 letter to his friend General Alexander McDougall, he complained, "All of you will be immortallising your selves in the golden pages of History, while I am confined to a series of [drudgeries] to pave the way for it."

Nevertheless, Greene performed the job of quartermaster general—and performed it quite effectively. It was a thankless job filled with frequent frustrations. Congress often meddled in the management of the quartermaster's department and balked at providing the necessary funds. Some American businessmen tried to fill their army contracts with inferior supplies and equipment in order to make extra money. And political enemies of Greene spread accusations of *profiteering* on the part of the quartermaster general. Greene, who valued his reputation highly, found these charges especially painful. Yet in spite of his desire for glory on the battlefield, and in spite of the attacks on his honor and the arguments with Congress, Nathanael Greene stayed on the job as quartermaster general for more than two years. He finally resigned in July 1780. His efforts helped transform the Continental Army into a force that had the material means to fight the British.

AN IMPROVED SHOWING BY THE CONTINENTALS

Greene's essential contributions in solving the army's supply and organizational crisis were evident long before 1780, though. Soon after leaving its encampment at Valley Forge in June 1778, the Continental Army stood up to crack British regulars in a pitched battle—and sent the British limping away. In addition to being better equipped thanks

Friedrich Wilhelm von Steuben was an experienced military officer from Prussia, an area of modern Germany that during the 18th century had one of the best-trained armies in Europe. During the winter at Valley Forge, von Steuben taught the Continental soldiers how to handle their weapons and maneuver on the battlefield—training that would pay dividends in the battles to come.

to Greene's efforts, the army was now better trained and more disciplined as a result of drilling it had received from Friedrich Wilhelm von Steuben, a Prussian military officer who had appeared at Valley Forge in February and volunteered his services.

Upon receiving news that France had decided to support the United States militarily, the new British commander, Sir Henry Clinton, decided to evacuate Philadelphia. Clinton didn't want to risk being bottled up in the city by a French fleet blocking the Delaware River. With a long column of redcoats and **Loyalists** on the march from Philadelphia to New York, Washington and his generals waited for an opportunity to strike. That opportunity came on June 28, 1778, when the Americans attacked the rear guard of the British column at Monmouth Court House, New Jersey. Clinton turned his army around for a massive counterattack. Elite British and Hessian units commanded by Charles

George Washington rallies his troops at the Battle of Monmouth, June 28, 1778. Greene played an important part in the battle, commanding Continental soldiers on the right side of the American line and repulsing furious attacks by elite British and Hessian units.

Cornwallis twice launched headlong attacks against the Continental units Nathanael Greene rushed forward to support the faltering right of the American line. Twice the British were repulsed. Savage fighting raged throughout the brutally hot day. But in the end, the Americans withstood everything the British threw at them—including the redcoats' most feared tactic, the bayonet attack. In the middle of the night, Clinton's battered troops slipped away and continued their march to New York City.

A BRIEF TIME HOME

By July, Washington had moved his army to White Plains, New York, to prevent a British advance up the Hudson River. At the end of the month, he sent Nathanael Greene home to Rhode Island to assist General John Sullivan in an upcoming offensive there. The Americans—in combination with the recently arrived French fleet—hoped to oust the British from Newport, which they had occupied since December 1776.

Before attending to his military responsibilities, Greene went to Spell Hall to see his family. Caty, who had spent the previous winter at the army's encampment in Valley Forge, was pregnant with the couple's third child. George was now three and Martha one. Unfortunately, their father was only able to remain in Coventry for about a week.

But the joint French-American offensive never materialized. After his fleet sustained damage during a two-day storm, the French commander insisted on retiring to Boston for repairs. General Sullivan reacted angrily, damaging relations with the French. A battle was fought on Aquidneck Island on August 29. Although the Americans—especially those under Greene's command—fought bravely and well, they couldn't hope to dislodge the British without French ships and troops. The Rhode Island campaign had to be abandoned.

By October 1778, Greene had to leave Rhode Island to select a suitable place for Washington's army to winter. He bade farewell to his family. He would not see Spell Hall again until 1783.

6

"WE FIGHT, GET BEAT, RISE AND FIGHT AGAIN"

The final months of 1778 and all of the following year passed with relatively little action between the main American and British armies. The British continued to hold New York City as their main base, while Washington kept his army nearby in case Clinton attempted a breakout. But neither commander was willing to risk an all-out offensive, so a tense stalemate resulted.

The standoff wasn't altogether bad news for the American cause: the British hadn't been able to deliver a knockout blow. But the Continental Army still teetered on the brink of collapse. Much of the blame lay with Congress. It still wasn't providing adequate supplies, instead relying on the individual states to outfit the soldiers raised within their borders. The winter of 1779–80, which the army spent in Morristown, New Jersey, was an especially grim time. Severe weather, shortages of food and clothing, and the failure of the soldiers to receive their pay caused morale to plummet. Men deserted in droves. Somehow, though, Washington and Greene managed to keep the army together.

With the war at a stalemate in the North, General Henry Clinton decided to focus British efforts on recapturing the southern colonies. Overwhelming American defenders they outnumbered four to one, the British took Savannah, Georgia, in December 1778 (above). The following year, French and American forces failed to recapture the city. After the withdrawal of the French and Americans, Clinton moved to consolidate British control in Georgia, then turned to South Carolina.

THE BRITISH LOOK SOUTHWARD

While the Continentals suffered through the bitter winter at Morristown, Sir Henry Clinton was preparing a campaign to strangle the rebellion. With the situation in the North stalemated, Clinton decided to invade the South. His strategy was simple: defeat the American forces in the southern states, restore those states to the Crown, and then proceed northward. Earlier, when a small British task force had taken Savannah, the capital of Georgia, Loyalists had rallied to the British. Now Clinton expected a similar reaction once the American army had been defeated on the battlefield.

In late December 1779, more than 8,500 of Clinton's best troops boarded ships and left New York for South Carolina. The British landed 30 miles south of Charleston, South Carolina's capital, in February 1780. The Americans made the disastrous decision to defend the city in the face of a British siege. On May 12, the American commander, Benjamin Lincoln, surrendered Charleston and its garri-

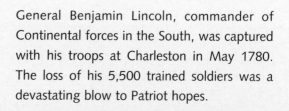

General Benjamin Lincoln, commander of Continental forces in the South, was captured with his troops at Charleston in May 1780. The loss of his 5,500 trained soldiers was a devastating blow to Patriot hopes.

Over Washington's objections, Congress chose General Horatio Gates (right), the hero of Saratoga, to take charge of the Southern Department of the Continental Army. Washington had suggested Nathanael Greene for the post.

son of more than 5,000 Continental soldiers and militiamen.

With the success of his strategy now seemingly ensured, Clinton returned to New York, leaving Charles Cornwallis in charge of subduing the rest of the South. Cornwallis unleashed a young *dragoon* commander, Lieutenant Colonel Banastre Tarleton, who quickly gained a reputation for ruthlessness. On May 29, at Waxhaw Creek, South Carolina, soldiers under the command of "Bloody Ban" massacred more than 100 Virginia Continentals who were attempting to surrender or had already surrendered.

As the direness of the situation in the South became apparent, Congress appointed a replacement for Benjamin Lincoln as commander of the Southern Department of the Continental Army. George Washington believed strongly that Nathanael Greene was the best man for the job, but Congress instead chose Major General Horatio Gates. Gates was considered the hero of Saratoga, but in reality much of the credit for that Continental victory should have belonged to General Benedict Arnold.

Shortly after taking command in the South, the over-confident Gates decided to engage Cornwallis in an all-out battle. He believed he could deal the British a decisive defeat. Instead, on August 16, 1780, Cornwallis smashed Gates's army of 1,500 Continentals and 1,500 militiamen at Camden, South Carolina. As the British charged and the

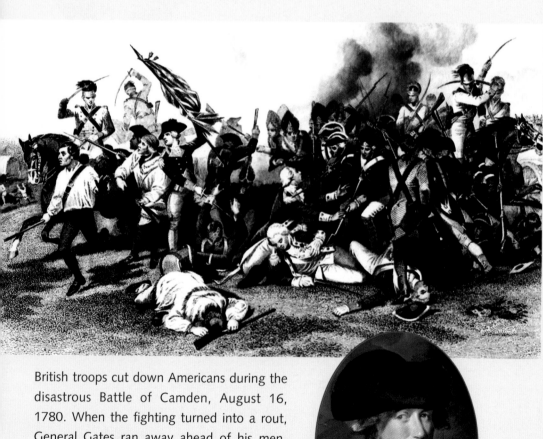

British troops cut down Americans during the disastrous Battle of Camden, August 16, 1780. When the fighting turned into a rout, General Gates ran away ahead of his men. The crushing defeat destroyed his reputation and led to his removal as commander in the South. With the American army all but destroyed, British general Charles Cornwallis (inset) had an opportunity to reestablish royal control over South Carolina.

militia broke and ran, Gates himself jumped on his horse and fled, not even pausing until he was 60 miles away from the battlefield. Behind him he left an absolute disaster: more than 1,000 Americans killed and wounded, another 1,000 captured. In a single day, Horatio Gates had lost an entire army.

"I AM GIVING YOU A GENERAL"

In the aftermath of the Battle of Camden, Congress allowed George Washington to appoint a general to replace Gates as commander of the Southern Department. He chose Nathanael Greene. "I think I am giving you a General," Washington wrote to a member of Congress on October 23, "but what can a General do, without Men, without Arms, without Clothing, without Stores, without Provisions?"

Two and a half years earlier, when he was "taken out of the Line of splendor" to become quartermaster general, Greene had complained about losing the chance to immortalize himself in "the golden pages of History." Now he had that chance. In fact, the fate of the entire Revolution rested squarely on his shoulders. But, as the tone of Washington's October 23 letter suggests, the prospects for success seemed slim. For Greene, the responsibility must have been overwhelming. "My dear Angel," he wrote to his wife, "What I have been dreading has come to pass. His Excellency

General Washington by order of Congress has appointed me to the command of the Southern Army."

FORMULATING A PLAN

The newly appointed commander immediately recognized that he couldn't meet the British head-on, as Gates had attempted at Camden with such disastrous results. So he formulated an ingenious strategy that, while it went against the accepted military thinking of the day, would prove to be a blueprint for defeating a stronger enemy. "My first object," Greene informed Washington in a letter dated October 31, 1780, "will be to equip a flying Army to con-sist of about eight hundred horse and one thousand Infantry." This highly mobile army—joined when possible by the militia and supplemented by bands of Patriot *partisans* operating elsewhere in the South—would con-stantly harass the British. The Americans would strike and withdraw, never risking everything on a single engagement. The redcoats might hold the field at the end of most if not all of the battles, but they would pay a price for each victo-ry. If the British decided to pursue Greene's army to deliv-er a knockout blow, they would be lured away from their supply bases and into the Carolina backcountry. And, as Greene noted in his letter to Washington, the American army would "render it difficult for them to subsist in the interior country." In the end, Greene hoped, the bloodied and exhausted redcoats would lose their will to continue the fight.

Of course, Greene would have to make sure his men didn't lose their will to continue the fight. As the Rhode Islander traveled south to assume command of the southern army during the fall of 1780, Patriots had little to cheer about. Benedict Arnold, hero of the American victory at Saratoga, had gone over to the British side. Though his plan to surrender the strategic fort of West Point had failed, Arnold would soon lead a destructive British raid into Virginia. Farther south, the British had subdued Georgia and South Carolina, and most of the people in those states now seemed to support the Loyalist cause. North Carolina, too, appeared to be inclining toward the king. Emboldened by the British victories, Loyalists flocked to Tory militias. These militias attacked, terrorized, and often killed their Patriot neighbors.

Yet there was some good news for the supporters of American independence. Patriot partisans were fighting back against the Tory militias and the British, and some of these partisan groups boasted excellent commanders, such as Francis "the Swamp Fox" Marion, Andrew Pickens, and Thomas Sumter. In early October, Tory militiamen under the command of a British officer named Patrick "Bull Dog" Ferguson were dealt a major defeat by American mountain men at the Battle of King's Mountain. This defeat spurred

Lord Cornwallis, who had thrust into North Carolina, to draw his forces back into South Carolina to regroup at Camden.

GREENE TAKES COMMAND

The remnants of the American southern army were camped at Charlotte, North Carolina, when Nathanael Greene arrived to take command on December 2, 1780. They presented a rather pathetic sight—"a few ragged, half-starved troops in the wilderness," Greene would say in a letter. There was only about three days' supply of food on hand, and the men had barely enough ammunition to fight a minor skirmish.

But Greene didn't wait for the situation to improve. He quickly decided on an extremely bold course of action: he would divide his badly outnumbered and ill-equipped force, sending a detachment of about 600 troops into western South Carolina while he marched the rest of the army into the northeastern part of the state, some 120 miles away. Greene's decision violated the accepted rules of military strategy, which said that a commander should never split his force in the face of a stronger enemy. But Greene recognized that Cornwallis couldn't fling his whole army at the detachment in the west without leaving the way open to Charleston for the American army in the east. And an all-out attack on Greene in the east would leave British forts in central South Carolina vulnerable to the American detachment in the west.

Greene's commander in the west was a tough Virginia backwoodsman named Daniel Morgan. The 45-year-old brigadier general had already distinguished himself as one of the Americans' ablest and most inspiring battlefield leaders. But his greatest victory lay ahead.

When reports of the American movements reached him, Lord Cornwallis marched his army north to engage the Continentals. Greene's decision to split his forces compelled Cornwallis to do the same. While he searched for the main body of the American army, Cornwallis dispatched a large force under the command of Banastre Tarleton to destroy Morgan's detachment in the west.

Tarleton commanded approximately 1,100 dragoons and light infantry soldiers. Morgan had about 600 Continental regulars and 200 to 400 state militiamen at his disposal. On January 17, 1781, the two forces collided in the rolling fields and pastures of a place called Cowpens. Morgan had chosen the

As commander in the South, Greene was blessed with excellent officers, including Brigadier General Daniel Morgan (shown here).

ground and deployed his men carefully, and he dealt the hated Bloody Ban one of the most crushing defeats of the entire war. After about an hour's fighting, 110 redcoats lay dead, and the 200 wounded were among more than 700 British soldiers taken prisoner.

When he learned of the disaster at the Battle of Cowpens, Cornwallis was furious. With about 2,500 men under his personal command, he set out to annihilate Morgan himself. Then he would descend on Greene and end the war in the South once and for all. To enable his column to move faster, Cornwallis decided to burn unnecessary equipment, provisions, and wagons. When informed of what the British

Continental soldiers overwhelm the British 7th Regiment of Foot during the final stages of the Battle of Cowpens.

commander had done by Light Horse Harry Lee's cavalry scouts, Greene is said to have exclaimed, "Then he is ours!"

In fact, the outcome was not yet settled. Greene still had to reunite his divided force while keeping ahead of the pursuing Cornwallis. With the British on their heels, Greene's and Morgan's troops retreated northward through North Carolina. Greene's experience as quartermaster general, along with his genius for planning and organization, would prevent disaster on more than one occasion during this frantic retreat. After being named commander of the Southern Department, Greene had quickly realized the significance of the many rivers and creeks in the Carolinas. He had ordered detailed surveys, and he knew where the waterways could be crossed. He also saw to it that boats were in place along the course of his planned retreat. In early February, Cornwallis believed he had Greene trapped on the southern banks of the deep Yadkin River. But when the redcoats arrived at the Yadkin, they realized that all the boats in the area, along with the Americans, were already on the other side.

RETREAT TO THE DAN

On February 9, the entire American army finally reunited at Guilford Courthouse, North Carolina. Greene's troops numbered around 1,500 Continental regulars and about 600 militiamen. The question was, should the Americans turn and fight, or should they continue the retreat? Though it meant giving up North Carolina for the time being, Greene chose the second option. If he could lead his men another 70 miles across the Dan River just over the North Carolina–Virginia border, they could rest and resupply in southern Virginia. Meanwhile, as Cornwallis continued the chase, the British would be moving farther and farther from their supply bases, over rugged terrain, and this would exhaust them.

On February 10, the bulk of the American army started for the Dan River. To slow Cornwallis down, Greene left behind a 700-man detachment under the command of Colonel Otho Williams. Despite Williams's harassment of the British column, Cornwallis managed to get troops into a position to block the only place he believed Greene could cross the Dan. Again, though, the British commander's designs were thwarted by the former quartermaster general. Greene had arranged for boats to be waiting at a site downriver from the British position, and the Americans safely crossed the Dan on February 14.

Cornwallis withdrew to Hillsborough, North Carolina. While Francis Marion and other Patriot partisans

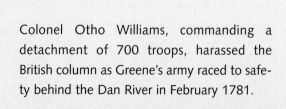

Colonel Otho Williams, commanding a detachment of 700 troops, harassed the British column as Greene's army raced to safety behind the Dan River in February 1781.

continued to carry out raids and hit-and-run attacks, Cornwallis could at least take comfort in having chased the American regular army from North Carolina. The British commander planned to mop up the Patriot resistance and restore North Carolina to the king's rule. He underestimated the resolve of the Fighting Quaker of Rhode Island.

CRIPPLING CORNWALLIS: THE BATTLE OF GUILFORD COURTHOUSE

On February 22, after little more than a week's rest, Nathanael Greene led his resupplied 1,600-man army back across the Dan and into North Carolina. Soon militia and Continental reinforcements from Virginia and North Carolina arrived, swelling Greene's force to more than 4,400 men. Cornwallis, whose remaining army totaled approximately 2,000, was now outnumbered. Still, Greene didn't immediately attack. Instead he kept his army on the move, forcing Cornwallis's tired troops to chase day after day, and bleeding the redcoats in numerous skirmishes.

Finally, on March 14, 1781, Greene marched his army back to Guilford Courthouse, where he intended to fight Cornwallis. Around 1:30 P.M. the following day, after a 12-mile march, the British column approached Guilford on New Garden Road. Greene had deployed his men in three lines. The first line, which straddled New Garden Road, was made up of about 1,000 North Carolina militiamen,

Greene's least reliable troops. About 300 yards to the rear, just inside some woods, was the second line. It was composed of 1,200 Virginia militia members. More than 500 yards behind this line, atop a low ridge overlooking a boot-shaped clearing, were Greene's best soldiers: more than 1,400 Continentals from Virginia, Maryland, and Delaware.

The British, hungry and weary but determined, formed their ranks and pressed forward. The North Carolina militia fired a volley. But the sight of battle-hardened British troops advancing for a bayonet attack caused most of them to run.

In this painting of the Battle of Guilford Courthouse, Maryland Continentals charge the British 2nd Guards with fixed bayonets. "I never saw such fighting since God made me," Lord Cornwallis later wrote of the March 15, 1781, battle. More than one-quarter of Cornwallis's men were killed or wounded in two hours of fighting.

Greene's second line did not give way so easily. For about a half hour, savage and confused fighting raged in the woods before the first British units began to emerge into the clearing in front of the last American line. Without waiting for all his comrades to get through the woods, a lieutenant colonel named James Webster led three British units in a charge at the Continental positions. Exposing himself to British fire, Greene rode along his line and shouted, "Be firm and steady! And give the finishing blow!"

The Continentals unleashed a deadly barrage that sent Webster and his men reeling back. But another British battalion, the elite 2nd Guards, soon cleared the woods and broke part of the American line. Before the Guards could push too far, however, Virginia horsemen under the command of George Washington's cousin William Washington swept behind them and charged through their ranks. As Washington's mounted troops slashed away with their sabers, Maryland Continentals pressed forward with fixed bayonets.

By this time, Cornwallis himself had crossed through the woods and into the clearing. Sensing that the Guards were about to be overrun—and that the entire battle would then be lost—Cornwallis made a controversial decision. He ordered his artillery to fire into the battle lines, knowing full well that British as well as American soldiers would be cut down. Cornwallis's pitiless action stopped the American onslaught, and he began re-forming his troops to press forward.

Now Nathanael Greene had a critical decision to make. He could mount a massive counterattack. If that attack succeeded, he might completely destroy Cornwallis's army. But if it failed, the American army—and with it, the whole Patriot cause—might be lost. At about 3:30 P.M., Greene ordered his troops to pull back, leaving the field to Cornwallis.

The British commander could thus claim victory at the Battle of Guilford Courthouse. But the price Cornwallis had paid was higher than he could afford. His casualties exceeded 500—more than one-quarter of his entire army. These included close to 100 men killed on the battlefield and an additional 40 who died of their wounds before the day was over. American losses, meanwhile, totaled about 400 men.

Three days after the battle, tired of war and longing to return to Spell Hall, Nathanael Greene wrote to Caty, "I should be extreeme happy if the war had an honorable close; and I on a farm with my little family about me. God grant the day may not be far distant, when peace with all her train of blessings, shall diffuse universal joy through America."

Peace would not be right around the corner, as Greene hoped. But after Guilford Courthouse, the tide of war shifted to the American side. George Washington under-

These iron cannonballs were recovered from the battlefield at Guilford Court-house. Although technically a British victory, because Greene's army left the field, the battle fatally weakened Cornwallis's army—and paved the way for the ulti-mate triumph of the American cause.

stood the significance of the battle. In a letter of congratu-lation to Greene dated March 21, 1781, the commander in chief wrote, "You may be assured that your retreat before Lord Cornwallis is highly applauded by all Ranks and reflects much honor on your military abilities."

His forces completely spent, Cornwallis soon withdrew to the port city of Wilmington, North Carolina. There he hoped to rest and resupply his army with the support of the British navy.

WAR OF THE POSTS

Cornwallis's retreat to Wilmington offered Greene the chance to retake South Carolina and Georgia. Thus began what would be called the "War of the Posts"—as Greene,

Light Horse Harry Lee, and partisan leaders such as Francis Marion attacked the now-exposed line of British forts Cornwallis had set up between the key cities of Savannah, Charleston, and Wilmington. As other Patriot forces captured Fort Motte, Fort Granby, Orangeburg, and Augusta, Greene committed the main part of his army at the Battle of Hobkirk's Hill on April 25, then again at the Siege of Ninety-Six from May 22 through June 19, and again at the bloody Battle of Eutaw Springs on September 8. None of these engagements could be counted as victories. But in

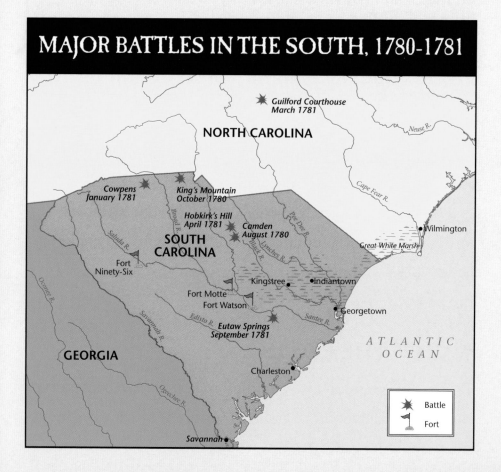

MAJOR BATTLES IN THE SOUTH, 1780-1781

Guilford Courthouse
March 1781

NORTH CAROLINA

Neuse R.

Cowpens
January 1781

King's Mountain
October 1780

Cape Fear R.

Hobkirk's Hill
April 1781

Camden
August 1780

Broad R.

Pee Dee R.

Lynches R.

Wilmington

Saluda R.

SOUTH CAROLINA

Black R.

Great White Marsh

Fort
Ninety-Six

Ocomee R.

Kingstree

Indiantown

Fort Motte
Fort Watson

Edisto R.

Eutaw Springs
September 1781

Santee R.

Georgetown

GEORGIA

Savannah R.

*A T L A N T I C
O C E A N*

Charleston

Ogeechee R.

Savannah

Battle

Fort

each case Greene exacted a heavy toll on the enemy, as he had at Guilford Courthouse. "We fight, get beat, rise and fight again," Nathanael Greene said. These simple words summed up the spirit of the Americans who fought in the southern campaign—and of their Rhode Island commander.

In April 1781, just as Greene was beginning his offensive in South Carolina, Cornwallis had decided to abandon Wilmington. He was, he wrote, "quite tired of marching about the country" in pursuit of Nathanael Greene. Instead, Cornwallis decided to take the fight to Virginia. That would prove to be a fateful decision. By early fall, Cornwallis found himself cornered at Yorktown, Virginia, by a French fleet, American troops under the command of George Washington, and a French expeditionary force led by General Jean Baptiste Donatien de Vimeur, comte de Rochambeau. On October 19, 1781, the British commander was forced to surrender his entire force of approximately 8,000.

7

A LIFE CUT SHORT

Although a peace treaty with Great Britain would not officially be concluded until September 3, 1783, the Revolutionary War was all but over by the spring of 1782. In late February of that year, Parliament passed a resolution urging the king to suspend the war. In April, Sir Guy Carleton replaced Sir Henry Clinton as the British commanding general, and he began the British withdrawal.

Nathanael Greene's southern campaign continued through 1782. The British, who had pulled out of North Carolina in early January, abandoned Savannah, Georgia, on June 11. On December 14, 1782, Greene—joined in victory by his wife, Catharine—marched his army into

Charleston, South Carolina, hours after the British commander had departed the city. The campaign to liberate the South, which Greene had begun two years earlier, was now complete.

On February 6, 1783, in a letter from his headquarters in Newburgh, New York, George Washington acknowledged the indispensable role his most trusted general had played in the American triumph. "I congratulate you," Washington wrote, "on the glorious end you have put to hostilities in the Southern States; the honour and advantage of it, I hope, and trust, you will live long to enjoy."

Greene's successful southern strategy forced Cornwallis to move his army north into Virginia, where he was trapped by French and American troops. The British general's surrender at Yorktown in October 1781, depicted in this painting, essentially marked the end of the American Revolution.

A NEW BEGINNING AND
A TRAGIC END

Tragically, Nathanael Greene did not live long to enjoy the honor and advantage of the victory he had done so much to secure. After resigning his commission in the Continental Army, he returned to Rhode Island. He turned Spell Hall over to his brother Jacob and moved Caty and their children for a time to Newport, Rhode Island. But his long-range plan was to settle in the South. The state of Georgia, in gratitude for Greene's efforts during the war, had awarded him a 2,141-acre plantation called Mulberry Grove. It was located on the Savannah River, just north of the city of Savannah.

Prominent Georgians encouraged Greene to become involved in politics, but he declined. A wartime business venture that failed had left Greene deeply in debt, and now he wanted to make money to secure his family's financial future. In addition to his plans to farm Mulberry Grove, he planned, along with his brother Jacob, to locate an expanded Greene family business in Charleston, South Carolina.

In October 1785, after renovations to the house at Mulberry Grove had been finished, Greene collected Caty and his five children and left Rhode Island for Savannah. Their excitement at going to a new home would soon be dampened by the loss of their sixth child, Catharine, who died shortly after her birth in Savannah.

By the following spring, the transplanted Rhode Islander was beginning to settle into the life of a southern planter. But on a blistering day in June, when he and Caty were visiting the plantation of their neighbor William Gibbons, Greene decided to join Gibbons on an hours-long ride over the grounds. He apparently suffered heatstroke as a result of the extended exposure to the blazing sun. After returning to Mulberry Grove, he went to bed, but his condition deteriorated. At 6:00 A.M. on Monday, June 19, 1786, Nathanael Greene died. He was 44 years old.

Nathanael Greene's untimely death meant that he didn't have the opportunity to participate in the political debates that led, in September 1787, to the drafting of the United States Constitution. Nor did Greene have the chance to serve in the administration of the nation's first president, George Washington—who almost certainly would have asked his loyal friend and trusted adviser to fill

For more than a decade after her husband's unexpected death in 1786, Caty Greene continued to live at Mulberry Grove, where she is said to have had a role in Eli Whitney's invention of the cotton gin. She died in 1814.

an important cabinet post. It is perhaps for these reasons that Americans today have largely forgotten the name of Nathanael Greene.

Yet Greene ranks among the most important figures of the American Revolution. No one besides George Washington did more to defeat the British in the field. When the cause of independence appeared lost, the Fighting Quaker of Rhode Island found the will, and the way, to prevail.

1742 Nathanael Greene is born in Potowomut, Rhode Island Colony, on July 27.

1754–1760 The French and Indian War is fought in North America. While Britain emerges victorious, the war leaves it deeply in debt.

1765 To help pay British war debts, Parliament passes the Stamp Act, which stirs anger in the American colonies. Nathanael Greene is sent to the village of Coventry to manage his family's iron forge there.

1767 Parliament imposes more unpopular taxes on the colonies with the Townshend Acts.

1770 On March 5, British soldiers kill five American rioters in an incident Patriots dub the Boston Massacre. Spell Hall, Nathanael Greene's home in Coventry, is completed; Greene's father dies.

1772 In February, the captain of the British naval vessel HMS *Gaspee* seizes a ship and cargo owned by Nathanael Greene and his brother. On June 10, Rhode Islanders burn the *Gaspee*.

1773 On the night of December 16, Patriots dump 342 cases of British tea into Boston Harbor in an incident that comes to be called the Boston Tea Party.

1774 Parliament passes the so-called Intolerable Acts. Greene helps form a militia unit, the Kentish Guard. On July 20, Greene marries Catharine Littlefield. In September, the First Continental Congress convenes in Philadelphia.

1775 On April 19, the battles of Lexington and Concord are fought, marking the beginning of the Revolutionary War. Nathanael and Catharine Greene's first child, George Washington Greene, is born. On May 8, Nathanael Greene is appointed brigadier general of the Rhode Island militia brigade. In June, Congress creates the Continental Army and appoints George Washington its commander; Greene is commissioned a brigadier general of the Continental Army. On June 17, the British win a costly victory at the Battle of Bunker Hill.

Chronology

1776   In March, the British abandon Boston. In April, the Continental Army marches to New York to defend against a British invasion. On July 4, the Continental Congress issues the Declaration of Independence. In August, Greene is promoted to the rank of major general. The British under Sir William Howe defeat the Americans at Long Island on August 27. On September 16, Greene helps lead a successful rear guard action at the Battle of Harlem Heights. On October 28, Howe defeats Washington at the Battle of White Plains. Greene's decision to defend Fort Washington ends with disaster when the British overwhelm the garrison on November 16. On December 26, Washington defeats the Hessians at the Battle of Trenton.

1777   On January 3, Washington defeats Lord Cornwallis at the Battle of Princeton. Nathanael and Catharine Greene's second child, Martha Washington Greene, is born. In August, Howe lands a large force at Head of Elk, Maryland, and begins his march on Philadelphia. On September 11, the British defeat Washington's army at the Battle of Brandywine; two weeks later, they march into Philadelphia unopposed. On October 17, the British general John Burgoyne surrenders his army at Saratoga, New York. In December, Washington's army marches to its winter camp in Valley Forge.

1778   In February, U.S. representatives led by Benjamin Franklin conclude a treaty of alliance with France in Paris. In March, Greene is appointed quartermaster general of the Continental Army. On June 28, after the British have abandoned Philadelphia, the Continental Army fights the British on equal terms at the Battle of Monmouth in New Jersey. Greene goes to Rhode Island to assist in a campaign that fails to materialize.

1779   The Greenes' third child, Cornelia, is born. The main British and American forces are locked in a stalemate around New York City. In December, a large British force under the command of Sir Henry Clinton sails out of New York, bound for South Carolina.

1780 The Greenes' son Nathanael is born. In February, Clinton's force lands south of Charleston. On May 12, Charleston surrenders. Clinton returns to New York, leaving Charles Cornwallis in charge in the South. On August 16, Cornwallis smashes the southern Continental Army under General Horatio Gates. Greene is appointed to succeed Gates as commander of the Southern Department; he officially takes command at Charlotte, North Carolina, on December 3.

1781 On January 17, Americans under Daniel Morgan rout a British force at the Battle of Cowpens in South Carolina. Greene conducts a brilliant retreat through North Carolina, crossing the Dan River in Virginia on February 14. On February 22, Greene moves his army back across the Dan and into North Carolina. On March 15, he cripples Cornwallis's army before retreating at the Battle of Guilford Courthouse. Cornwallis withdraws to Wilmington, North Carolina, before moving his force into Virginia. Greene's army, along with American militia and partisan forces, begins to retake North Carolina, South Carolina, and Georgia. On October 19, 1781, Cornwallis surrenders at Yorktown, Virginia.

1782 The British abandon Wilmington, North Carolina, in January; Savannah, Georgia, in June; and Charleston, South Carolina, in December.

1783 In August, with peace established, Greene leaves the South. On September 3, the Treaty of Paris is signed, officially ending the Revolutionary War. Greene resigns his commission and returns to Rhode Island.

1784 The Greenes' daughter Louisa is born.

1785 Greene moves his family from Rhode Island to Mulberry Grove, his plantation near Savannah, Georgia. The Greenes' daughter Catharine is born, but she dies in infancy.

1786 On June 19, Nathanael Greene, age 44, dies at Mulberry Grove from the effects of sunstroke.

Glossary

brigadier general—a commissioned officer in the army ranking above a colonel.

dragoon—in the 18th century, a soldier who rode a horse into battle but might fight on foot.

duties—taxes on imported goods.

foraging—the act of searching the countryside for food or supplies.

Hessians—German professional soldiers, or mercenaries, hired by the British to fight in the Revolutionary War.

Loyalist—an American colonist who supported the king during the Revolutionary War period; also called a Tory.

major general—a commissioned officer in the army ranking above a brigadier general.

militia—nonprofessional troops called upon to fight the enemy in times of emergency; during the Revolutionary War, they were considered highly unreliable.

Parliament—England's legislature, or lawmaking body.

partisan—a member of a band of irregular fighters operating behind the enemy's lines.

Patriots—Americans who opposed the king and favored independence during the Revolutionary War.

profiteering—the act of making unreasonably high profits on the sale of essential goods during war or other times of emergency, often through the misuse of an official position.

Quaker—a member of a Christian group, called the Society of Friends, that originated in England in the mid-1600s.

quartermaster general—a staff officer in charge of keeping the army supplied.

redcoat—a British soldier.

regular—a soldier who is a member of a standing army as opposed to a militia.

Tory—an American colonist who supported the king during the Revolutionary War period; also called a Loyalist.

Books for Students:

Bober, Natalie S. *Countdown to Independence: A Revolution of Ideas in England and Her American Colonies 1760–1776.* New York: Simon & Schuster, 2001.

Bobrick, Benson. *Fight for Freedom: The American Revolutionary War.* New York: Simon & Schuster, 2004.

Green, Carl R. *The Revolutionary War.* Berkeley Heights, N.J.: Enslow, 2002.

Hairr, John. *Guilford Courthouse: Nathanael Greene's Victory in Defeat, March 15, 1781.* Cambridge, Mass.: Da Capo Press, 2002.

Herbert, Janis. *The American Revolution for Kids: A History with 21 Activities.* Chicago: Chicago Review Press, 2002.

Murray, Stuart. *The American Revolution.* New York: DK Publishing, 2002.

Strum, Richard M. *Causes of the American Revolution.* Stockton, N.J.: OTTN Publishing, 2005.

Books for Older Readers:

Anderson, Lee Patrick. *Forgotten Patriot: The Life and Times of Major General Nathanael Greene.* Boca Raton, Fla.: Universal Publishers, 2002.

Golway, Terry. *Washington's General: Nathanael Greene and the Triumph of the American Revolution.* New York: Henry Holt and Co., 2005.

McCullough, David. *1776.* New York: Simon & Schuster, 2005.

Roberts, Cokie. *Founding Mothers: The Women Who Raised Our Nation.* New York: HarperCollins, 2004.

Stegeman John F., and Janet A. Stegeman. *Caty: A Biography of Catharine Littlefield Greene.* Athens: University of Georgia Press, 1977.

Internet Resources

http://www.geocities.com/Pentagon/3901/index2.html

The Official General Nathanael Greene History & Museum at Spell Hall Website: By Gregg A. Mierka & Neal Demers

http://members.aol.com/JonMaltbie/NatGreene.html

General Nathanael Greene Biography: By Michael D. Kennedy

http://www.americanrevwar.homestead.com/files/
GREENE.HTM

General Nathanael Greene Biography: By George A. Billias and Edward P. Hamilton

http://virtualology.com/nathanaelgreene.net/

General Nathanael Greene Biography: By Stan Klos

http://sciway3.net/clark/revolutionarywar/cp12.html

Greene Assumes Command: By Dr. Frank O. Clark

http://www.nps.gov/revwar

National Park Service Revolutionary War Site

Numbers in **bold italics** refer to captions.

Index

Page:

2:	Collection of William Maxwell Greene; photo by Gregg A. Mierka	52:	Library of Congress
8-9:	Michael Dunn	55:	From *The Story of the Revolution* by Henry Cabot Lodge
8:	Library of Congress	56:	Independence National Historical Park
13:	Photo by Gregg A. Mierka		
16:	Library of Congress	57:	Independence National Historical Park
18:	Photo by Gregg A. Mierka		
20:	"Burning of the Gaspee," Charles DeWolf Brownell, from the Collections of the Rhode Island Historical Society	58:	(top) National Archives; (bottom) Charles, 1st Marquess Cornwallis (1738-1805) (gouache on paper) by Gardner, Daniel (1750-1805) © Private Collection/The Bridgeman Art Library
23:	Library of Congress	63:	Independence National Historical Park
26:	Library of Congress		
29:	Collection of the Fort Ticonderoga Museum	64:	Paintings by Don Troiani, www.historicalartprints.com
31:	Library of Congress	66:	Independence National Historical Park
33:	Library of Congress		
37:	US Senate Collection		
39:	© OTTN Publishing	68:	From *The Story of the Revolution* by Henry Cabot Lodge
41:	Library of Congress		
43:	"The Attack upon the Chew House," from *The Story of the Revolution* by Henry Cabot Lodge (1850-1924), published in Scribner's Magazine by Pyle, Howard (1853-1911) © Delaware Art Museum, Wilmington, USA/ The Bridgeman Art Library	71:	Courtesy National Park Service, Museum Management Program and Guilford Courthouse National Military Park, Iron D 10.3cm GUCO 99, Iron D 9cm GUCO 133, Iron D 7.1cm GUCO 11, Iron D 6cm GUCO 145, www.cr.nps.gov/museum
46:	© OTTN Publishing	72:	© OTTN Publishing
47:	Library of Congress	75:	Architect of the Capitol
49:	Library of Congress	77:	Courtesy of Gregg A. Mierka
51:	Independence National Historical Park	88:	Photo by M.V. Mierka

Front Cover: "Major General Nathanael Greene," by James Ward, 39" x 31 1/2", collection of the Nathanael Greene Homestead, Spell Hall Museum, Rhode Island; photo by Gregg A. Mierka

Back Cover: Collection of William Maxwell Greene; photo by Gregg A. Mierka

Acknowledgments

This book is dedicated to the memory and greatness of Nathanael Greene of Spell Hall, Coventry, Rhode Island, hero of the American Revolution, and Major General ~ United States Continental Army, who served under the Command of His Excellency, Commander-in-Chief, Lieutenant General George Washington. Thank you for the research assistance given by Mary Mierka and Thomas Enoch Greene, President of the Nathanael Greene Homestead Museum Association, Spell Hall, for permission to illustrate this book with never-before-published images, including the painting of General Nathanael Greene by artist James Ward. A special acknowledgment must also go to Mary, Robert, Barbara and Lori Mierka for their faith, love and devotion to this humble writer. Thank you also to James Gallagher, Lee Patrick Anderson, Michael Hill and David McCullough for your inspiration.

In writing this book author Gregg A. Mierka felt a strong sense of kinship with his friends and Greene history mentors Thomas Enoch Greene, Thomas Casey Greene and Robert Allen Greene, as well as a feeling of gratitude for the pens of Nathanael Greene, George Washington Greene, George Sears Greene, and Francis Vinton Greene.

About the Author

GREGG A. MIERKA was born in Detroit, Michigan, in 1950, and currently lives on the grounds of the General Nathanael Greene Homestead Museum, Spell Hall, in Coventry, Rhode Island. Mr. Mierka and his wife, Mary, were married in 1972. Since 1995, they have conducted the tours and education programs at Spell Hall, which is the historic 1770 home of General Nathanael Greene. Mr. Mierka is a graduate of Central Michigan University (1972 and 1974), Rhode Island School of Design (1980), and Harvard University (1984). For several years Mr. Mierka also taught at primary and secondary schools and colleges in Michigan, New York, and Rhode Island. As a painter, Mr. Mierka's works have been exhibited in America as well as Europe, and are among several public and private collections. He also worked for film director Ronald Maxwell on the movie *Gettysburg* as part of assistant director Skip Cosper's Corps of Civil War Specialists under historian Brian Pohanka, co-producer of the *A&E Civil War Journal*. After completion of *Gettysburg*, he worked on the French and Indian/Revolutionary War film *The Broken Chain*. In 2004, Mr. Mierka provided information about Nathanael Greene to author-historian David McCullough as part of his research for the book *1776*. Other works by Mierka are his series of biographies called *Rhode Island's Own*, combined with transcripts and personal narratives of Union soldiers and sailors who served in the Civil War compiled and written for the Military Order of the Loyal Legion of the United States. He is currently working on part three of the series *The Life of Colonel Elisha Hunt Rhodes*, with Robert Hunt Rhodes, Elisha's grandson and author of the book *All for the Union*.